D1744399

Ethical Dialogue

with

Other Religions

by

Myrtle Langley

Tutor in Missiology at Trinity College, Bristol

GROVE BOOKS

BRAMCOTE   NOTTS.

CONTENTS

NOTE ON TRANSLITERATION

Certain Indian words on pages 14-15 have been transliterated into English characters under the limitations of the typefaces available, and without the long accent (as in 'ō') appearing over the letters 'a' and 'u'.

First Impression January 1979

ISSN 0305 4241

ISBN 0 905422 50 3

I THE CHRISTIAN ETHIC AND OTHER RELIGIONS

1. The Imperative of Love

The Christian imperative is a law of love: to love God and to love one's neighbour. From the outset, however, it raises at least one definitional question of immense significance for Christians in Britain today: 'Who is my neighbour?'

(i) Who is my neighbour?

Human beings are social animals. It is characteristic of the species to form 'in groups' and 'out groups'. Indeed, all ancient and so-called primitive cultures draw a line of distinction between inside and outside, applying one set of laws to those inside and another to those outside. Take, for example, the ancient Greeks and the Israelites.

In the world of the ancient Greeks one's 'neighbour' is the person who lives nearby, the 'person next door' and only by extension does the term eventually denote one's 'fellow man' generally.[1]

In the Septuagint (the Greek version of the Old Testament) the same Greek word is used extensively to translate a Hebrew word meaning basically the 'person with whom one has dealings', an 'associate'.[2]

In the Deuteronomic Law and the Holiness Code the legal statutes are expressly related to the fact of Israel's election as the people of God. Thus, according to Leviticus 19.18 the command to love one's neighbour applies unequivocally towards members of Yahweh's covenant community and not self-evidently to those outside—towards all men. However, it is true that Leviticus 19.34 imposes an obligation towards the strangers who sojourn in the land: 'The stranger who sojourns with you shall be to you as the native among you, and you shall love him as yourself; for you were strangers in the land of Egypt: I am the Lord your God' (cf. Deut. 10.19).

This use of 'sojourner' in the commandment of love makes possible extension on the one hand and restriction on the other. While, strictly-speaking, a distinction is made between the elect—members of the covenant community who share in its implied duties and rights—and those outside, no such distinction is made in practice. Because obligations are imposed towards strangers dwelling in the land the division between insiders and outsiders becomes essentially a matter of residence. If they hold residence in common all is well. Jewish exposition of a later period, however, presupposes an express limitation. The commandment applies only in relation to Israelites and full proselytes. Samaritans, foreigners and resident aliens who do not join the community of Israel within twelve months are excluded. Indeed, by the time of Jesus, exceptions abound: Pharisees are inclined to exclude all non-Pharisees, the masses of town and country dwellers for whom the law proved too cumbersome; the

---

1 The word *plesion* is used by Philo and in ethical discourses; cf. Heinrich Greeven in G. Kittel and G. Friedrich (eds), *Theological Dictionary of the New Testament.* Vol. VI (Eerdmans, Grand Rapids, 1968), pp.311-18.
2 The Hebrew word is *re'a*, ibid. Cf. I. Howard Marshall *The Gospel of Luke*, (Paternoster, Exeter, 1978) p.444.

strict sect of the Essenes exhorts its members to love only the children of light and hate the children of darkness; a rabbinical saying rules that heretics, informers and renegades 'should be pushed (into the ditch) and not pulled out'[1]; and a popular saying referrred to by Jesus commands the people to love their neighbours and hate their enemies.[2]

It helps in understanding this trend if we remember that a great deal more coming and going had developed and Gentiles—Romans, Syrians and Greeks among them—were to be found much more commonly in the land. By the time of Jesus the distinction between 'insider' and 'outsider' had become not a little difficult. And the increasing tendency to limitation most likely reflects the ensuing uncertainty. So there arises the conscious need to pose again the question: 'Who is my neighbour?' 'Who is my fellow man?'

Similarly, in Britain today, with people not only from other lands but of other races, cultures and religions in our midst, we are not certain as to who really belongs, as to who is on the inside. If, like the 'extensionists' in Israel, we apply only the criterion of residence, then all people living in Britain today whatever their race, class, colour or creed are insiders. But to most people this criterion is neither immediately apparent nor unequivocally acceptable. Not many of the rank and file of British people were consciously affected by the fact of empire nor are they any the more aware of the consequences of its loss, in terms of dislocation of peoples, either for the 'mother country' herself or her 'alien' subjects. It is not surprising that they feel themselves threatened, territorially, economically, and culturally, by an influx of strangers into the land. And like the restrictionists in Israel they respond by posing yet again the question: 'Who is in?', 'Who is my fellow countryman?', 'Who is my neighbour?', anticipating a reply, presumably, which will set bounds and apply limits.

When faced with this same question Jesus gives an unequivocal reply. By relating the parable of the Good Samaritan (Lk. 10.25-37) he turns the question round from focussing on objective definition to dealing with subjective relationship. Instead of answering the question 'Who is my neighbour?' and concerning himself with the object of love he answers the much more penetrating and demanding 'To whom can I be a neighbour?', concentrating on the subject of love. And his reply is devastating: in effect, 'My neighbour is anybody, anywhere, in need'. No longer is it adequate, implies Jesus, to be limited by categories, to know one's duties and to be bound by them, but rather to be motivated by love—love without limits and knowing no bounds.

(ii) Being a neighbour
Jesus countered the stance taken by the lawyers of his time not only by parable and by precept ('But I say to you, love your enemies and pray for those who persecute you' (Mt. 5.44)) but also by example. His attitude to 'foreigners' may be illustraced by his treatment of groups such as the Samaritans, the bordering peoples and the Gentiles generally.

---

1 Joachim Jeremias, TheP arables of Jesus (SCM, London, Revised Edition, 1963), pp.202-3; cf. H. Greeven, loc, cit.
2 Cf. Mt. 5.43 where Jesus is reported as saying, 'You have heard that it was said, "You shall love your neighbour and hate your enemy".'

Jesus spoke to the Samaritan woman at the well (Jn. 4.1-42), refused to call down fire from heaven on the unwelcoming Samaritan villagers (Lk. 9.51-6), singled out for commendation the 'foreign' Samaritan leper (Lk. 17.11-19) and, as if this were not enough, told a parable in which the hero was a 'good Samaritan' (Lk. 10.15-37). What this meant in terms of flouting convention and not being bound by the categories of his time can only be properly realized by taking a look at Jewish-Samaritan relations. There was a history of bad relations. Jews hated Samaritans because they were half-breeds—racially they were of mixed descent, religiously they were less than orthodox, indeed positively syncretistic—and Samaritans reciprocated. Moreover, between A.D. 6 and A.D. 9, during a Passover celebration, at midnight, the Samaritans defiled the Temple court by strewing it with dead men's bones and thereafter hostility became irreconcilable. As the Gospels repeatedly tell us: Jews had no dealings with Samaritans. In practice this meant excluding Samaritans from the Jerusalem cultus, not eating meat slaughtered for Samaritans, not partaking of their Passover and not using their drinking vessels[1]. In short, Jews treated Samaritans as enemies, and enemies were to be hated. What an extreme choice Jesus made then when he singled out Samaritans for attention and commended them as being worthy of praise and exemplary in conduct.

Likewise, Jesus responded favourably to the request of the Syro-phoenician woman whose daughter was ill (Mk. 7.24-30 and parallels) and to the centurion whose servant was paralyzed (Mt. 8.5-13).[2]

And so by precept, parable and example Jesus emphasizes the inwardness and inclusiveness of Christian love. Such love is no outward qualification (meriting eternal life) but rather an inner disposition: it is not a mere fulfilling of one's duty within certain defined limits but a way of life which embraces all sorts and conditions of men.

2. The Affirmation of Humanness
Love implies affirmation. We may properly ask what it was that Jesus affirmed when he treated so-called 'outsiders' with love and respect. I believe it was their humanness. According to biblical insights all people hold humanness in common.

(i) *The nature of our common humanity*
Our common humanity marks us out as one in origin and purpose, created by God to fulfil a role characterized by a threefold relationship: to God, nature and society. The same common humanity, however, marks us out as many dispersed peoples alienated in all three areas.

. . . (a) Creation and alienation
God created man (Gen. 2.7); he created him in his own image (Gen. 1.27); male and female he created them (Gen. 1.27). And God saw that everything which he had made was very good (Gen. 1.31).

---

1 Joachim Jeremias in G. Kittel and G. Friedrich (eds), *op. cit.*, Vol. VII, pp.90ff.
2 The Syro-phoenician woman was probably Greek-speaking or Greek in culture; the centurion belonged to the Roman occupying power and was thus the object of much nationalist-inspired hatred. (Cf. C. E. B. Cranfield, *The Gospel according to St Mark* (C.U.P., 1963), *ad loc.*).

Although the *nature* of God's image in man has often pre-occupied thinkers and been much in dispute, it would appear that its *purpose* is much more central to the concerns of the Genesis narrative.[1] In Genesis 1.28 we are informed of the command to man to 'subdue' and 'rule' the earth. By subjection is most probably meant the kind of activity by which man reduces the earth's resources to his own use (Josh. 18.1).[2] By 'rule' is most likely meant the refashioning activity such as is exemplified in the treading of the wine-press when grapes are turned into wine (Joel 3.13).[3] Consequently, by virtue of his creation by God in God's own image—with the declared purpose of his subduing and ruling the earth—man enjoys a special relationship with God and nature. His is a mediating role of being God's appointed steward on the earth: man is responsible to God for the rest of creation. Thus, a unique relationship is established between man and God and between man and nature. But a third relationship is also envisaged—a family relationship—of a man with members of his own species. As Gerhard von Rad puts it: 'By God's will man was not created alone but designated for the "thou" of the other sex.'[4] Man was destined to fill the earth as well as to rule and subdue it.

In sum, man's creation in God's image establishes a triad of relationships embracing God, nature and society.

However, as we have already had cause to note, our common humanity also marks us out as universally alienated in all three relationships. Biblically speaking, it is not man's appointed task in the world which is vitiated by sin but rather his ability to fulfil it. Relationships between man and God, man and wife, man and nature are broken by disobedience on man's part (Gen. 3 *passim*). Moreover, it is important to note that neither child-bearing nor work in themselves constitute the punishment for sin, but rather the difficulty with which they will have to be performed. Procreation and work are man's destiny; pain in childbearing and difficulty in subjecting and ruling the earth are alienating and man's punishment for sin.[5]

. . . (b) Unity and dispersion

When Paul states in Acts 17.26 that God 'made from one every nation of men to live on all the face of the earth' he is countering from a biblical standpoint the Athenian belief that they had 'sprung from the soil of their

[1] Gerhard von Rad, *Genesis* (SCM, London, 1961), pp.56ff.: 'One will admit that the text speaks less of the nature of God's image than of its purpose. There is less said about the gift itself than about the task. This then is sketched most explicitly: domination in the world, especially over the animals.'

[2] The Hebrew is *kibsuha*. Cf. Hans Walter Wolff, *Anthropology of the Old Testament* (SCM, London, 1973), pp.159-65. Wolff notes the use of *kbs* for the subjection of a country through war (Num. 32.22, 29), the subjection of peoples (2 Sam. 8.1) and of slaves particularly (Neh. 5.5), also the raping of women (Esther 7.8) but with the special meaning of 'an action in which man reduces something to his use through the application of force' (Josh. 18.1).

[3] The Hebrew is *re' du*, cf. ibid. *Rdh* is applied to king's rule in Ps. 72.8; Ps. 110.2; Is. 14.6 and Ezek. 34.4. But Wolff would see the rule granted to all men, and the meaning as perhaps developed from 'to tread' in the sense of Joel 4.13 where the treading of the grapes in the winepress is described.

[4] Von Rad, *op. cit.*, p.58.

[5] *Ibid.*, p.78.

native Attica'.[1] By so doing he is denying the Greek claim to racial superiority over the so-called 'barbarians'. Mankind, says Paul, has one source— in God the Creator.

The story of Babel as recorded in Genesis 11.1-9 is a piece of human cultural history in which 'man's rebellion against God becomes evident and in which God's judgment took place'.[2] The rebellion took the form of mankind's striving for fame, alliance and political development, all of which set him, in his pride, against God. The judgment which followed entailed the scattering into disorder and mutual incomprehension of those who so sought 'unity' and alliance. Thus, the final judgment on what may be called 'the continually widening chasm between man and God' (as evident in the early chapters of Genesis) was the Dispersion, the dissolution of mankind's unity. Concludes von Rad, pertinently, on this point: 'The multitude of nations indicates not only the manifold quality of God's creative power but also a judgment, for the disorder in the international world, which our narrative regards as the sad conclusion, was not willed by God but is punishment for the sinful rebellion against God'.[3]

. . . (c) Culture
The tension is now clear, for although man is alienated he still bears God's image in some sense, although dispersed and scattered in disorder he still belongs to one family. Consequently, the culture which he develops is at one and the same time stamped by the marks of creation and alienation, of unity and disorder.

By culture I mean:
(1)   *science and technology,* expressing specifically man's relationship to his physical environment;
(2)   *social system,* expressing man's efforts to relate to his human environment;
(3)   *religion or belief-system,* expressing specifically man's relation to God, ultimate reality, ultimate concern or the ground of his being— individual religions are particular social realizations of this relationship.

These components of culture are like three layers of a triangle:

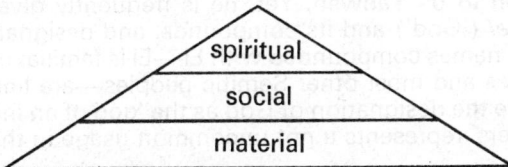

At the base is the first layer consisting of *material* artifacts; in the middle is the second layer comprising human institutions, or the *social* dimension; at the apex is the third layer made up of values, ideologies, cosmologies, world views—the *spiritual* dimension. Each ascending layer becomes increasingly complex and abstract.

1 F. F. Bruce, *The Acts of the Apostles: The Greek Text with Introduction and Commentary* (Tyndale Press, London, 21952), pp.336-7; J. Rawson Lumby, *The Acts of the Apostles* (C.U.P., 1882), p.228.
2 Von Rad, *op. cit.,* p.147.
3 *Ibid.,* p.148.

Bearing the stamp of creation and including as it does so much that is vital and necessary to man's existence, culture is in many ways good and enriching. But, conversely, bearing the stamp of man's alienation, it also contains much that is evil and impoverishing. Indeed, it is for the latter reason, so Paul informs us, that God gives man over to his own corrupted mind (cf. Rom. 1.24).[1]

(ii) *Salvation history*

. . . *(a) The cultural and the supracultural*

There is something to be said for a distinction which has been made between the cultural and the supracultural.[2] By the *cultural* is meant those phenomena, material and non-material, which have been developed by man. There are some 3,500 distinct ethnic groups in the world, each one possessing a different cultural system developed by men and passed on from one generation to the next. Within each group the cultural system gives integration and order to life. However, culture is essentially man-made and because man is alienated from God culture reflects this alienation in its man-centred concerns and perspectives. Each succeeding generation then inherits cultural patterns reflecting not only man's quest for God but his alienation also. By the *supracultural* is meant those phenomena which have their source outside the sphere of culture but which, nonetheless, can penetrate it and find expression in it. Two such sources may be postulated: that which stems from God—the gospel, faith, the work and fruit of the Spirit, etc.; and that which stems from Satan—evil, unbelief, sin etc.

This distinction between the *cultural* and the *supracultural* spheres is, of course, a theoretical one. And to distinguish between that which in essence is determined by God's activity (the supracultural) and that which is man's response (the cultural) is difficult. Yet, in trying to distinguish between religion and faith, revelation and religion, I have found the distinction extremely helpful, as for example in the case of Abraham.

. . . *(b) Revelation and religion*

To a man in the cultural milieu of the ancient Near East came a special revelation. The Genesis narrative unquestionably considers the bearer of this revelation to be Yahweh. Yet, he is frequently given other divine names such as *el* ('God') and its compounds, and designated the 'god of the fathers'. The names compounded with El—El is familiar as the high-god of the Canaanites and most other Semitic peoples—are linked to specific cultic sites, while the designation of God as the 'god of an individual' or the 'god of the fathers' represents a not uncommon usage in the ancient Near East.[3]

---

[1] See C. E. B. Cranfield, *The Epistle to the Romans,* Vol. 1 (T. & T. Clark, Edinburgh, 1975), pp.121-2. I am sympathetic to Cranfield's suggestion that God 'delivers up' as 'an act of judgment and mercy on the part of God who smites in order to heal' (Is. 19.22) and that throughout a time of God-forsakenness God is still concerned with these people and dealing with them.

[2] G. Linwood Barney, 'The Supracultural and the Cultural Implications for Frontier Missions', in R. Pearce Beaver (ed.), *The Gospel and Frontier Peoples: A Report of a Consultation December 1972* (William Carey Library, Pasadena, 1973), pp. 48-57.

[3] See Helmer Ringgren, *Israelite Religion* (SPCK, London, 1966), pp.17-27, particularly pp.19-21.

It appears to me very likely that belief in a unique combination of personal, tribal and elemental divinity prepared Abraham for God's revelation to him. At this point the supracultural was to invade the cultural, revelation was to take over from religion. Man-centred culture was to be transformed and re-orientated to reflect the supracultural with its divine source. Or to put it in yet another way, the 'appointed time' had come for the manifestation of God to a chosen people.[1] For Abraham's faith was reckoned to him as righteousness (Gen. 15.6) and a covenant established between him and Yahweh. The covenant was extended to his descendants and thereby a particular people was chosen out to be God's own.

... (c) Law and grace

The establishment of the covenant was an indication of God's grace, the undeserved favour which he bestowed on each patriarch in turn and on a people in slavery in Egypt. Nonetheless, the history of the patriarchs and the twelve tribes of Israel demonstrated only too clearly the persistence of man's alienation and pointed up the need for something more. It was provided in the Sinaitic covenant, the basis of which became the Law, moral, cultic and social.

... (d) Incarnation and redemption

But even the Law in turn pointed up the need for a remedy more capable of dealing with man's alienation and dispersion. Says Paul: 'If it had not been for the law, I should not have known sin . . . But sin, finding opportunity in the commandment, wrought in me all kinds of covetousness . . . the very commandment which promised life proved to be death to me' (Rom. 7.7-10). It was met this time in the gift of God's Son who himself became man. The Second Adam became the bearer and head of the new humanity (cf. Rom. 5.1-21; 2 Cor. 5.11-21).

But this man, Jesus Christ, became also the Redeemer, the first fruits of redemption (1 Cor. 15.20), a redemption which will culminate in the setting free of the whole creation and the redemption of men's bodies (cf. Rom. 8.22, 23).

Already, we have experienced something of the great reversal of redemption: by the cross man has been reconciled to God and God to man: at Pentecost the gospel was heard and understood by peoples of many different nations and languages; and in Christ's body, the church, there is neither Jew nor Greek, slave nor free, male nor female, because all are one in Christ Jesus (cf. Rom. 5.10, 11; Acts 2.6; Gal. 3.28).

(iii) The implications of our common humanity

The foregoing has important implications and this is especially true for a culturally and ethnically pluralistic society.

---

[1] *Kairos* is the New Testament word for 'time'. According to Oscar Cullman (*Christ and Time* (SCM, London, Revised Edition, 1962), pp.39-40) *kairos*, whether in secular or New Testament usage, is the moment in time which is especially favourable for an undertaking. With reference to salvation history it is that aspect of time which has a special place in the execution of God's plan for salvation.

. . . (a) Solidarity

The nature of mankind's solidarity may be summarized in a series of propositions as follows:

(1) Although culturally, ethnically, and linguistically, devided, *mankind is in origin one.*

(2) God's purpose for mankind is one and the same, that *man should,* in special relationship with his Creator, *exercise responsible stewardship over creation.*

(3) *The creation, of which man is a part, was declared good by its Creator.*

(4) *All men participate in the curse* consequent upon man's irresponsible act of alienating himself from his Creator and creation.

(5) *All culture* (of which religion may be said to be a part) *is man's attempt to relate to his total environment:* spiritual, social and physical.

(6) However, because God did not abandon his universe (becoming transcendent and wholly other without at the same time becoming immanent and wholly man), but continued to uphold it and inaugurated its redemption (Col. 1.15-17; Rom. 8.18-25), *culture is stamped by much that is positively good and of God.*

(7) Indeed, *all men,* in some sense, *partake of the fruits both of God's redemptive and creative activity:* through Christ God was pleased to reconcile all things to himself (making peace by the blood of his cross (Col. 1.19-20)) and through Christ's body, the church, God is pleased to preserve the world from total destruction (Mt. 5.13-16). To quote but one example—God's healing activity is to be seen in the development of scientific medicine, whether the doctor be Christian or Hindu, Muslim or Sikh.

(8) Similarly, *all men,* whether Christian or non-Christian, *share in the ills of a sin-dominated, albeit God-originated, world.* Again, to quote but one example—although God's healing activity is manifestly evident in the development of scientific medicine so too is man's frequent abuse of his power and repeated mis-use of his responsibility.

(9) Therefore, *Christians,* in the awareness of their solidarity with sinful humanity and their inability to save themselves, *must forsake* their oftentimes overweening condemnation of or patronizing tolerance of other religions *and recognize the differences between religion, revelation, and revelation culturally clad:* even our Christian faith is culturally clad.

(10) Finally, Christians ought to be prepared for the possibility that as God was able to reveal himself to Abraham at the appointed time so too he may choose to reveal the fulness of Christ to men of other religions (for example, African Traditional Religions) at the point

when he considers them ready to receive the gospel. In this sense *non-Christian religions may be viewed as 'praeparatio evangelica' (preparation for the gospel),* but on no account must they be seen to replace the Old Testament Scriptures or be allowed to detract from the fulness and uniqueness of Christ.[1]

... (b) Dialogue

Solidarity implies dialogue (as two-way conversation). And on the basis of a model (which like all models must be allowed to have its limitations) dialogue may be said to occur at three distinct levels: of living, thinking and believing. The level of *believing* involves *theology,* the level of *thinking epistemology* or philosophy of religion and the level of *living anthropology* or common humanity, what Bishop Kenneth Cragg calls 'participation in the human condition . . . the common denominator'.[2]

3. The Necessity of Understanding

Comparative religionists of the not-too-distant past were fond of selecting various tenets of belief and placing them alongside each other, drawing contrasts and making comparisons. The employment of such methods is now out of fashion and rightly so. Of much greater value is the phenomenological or empathetic approach, an adaptation of which I seek to employ in my own thinking and teaching.[3] It is a modification of what John S. Dunne calls 'passing over' and which he describes as follows:

'Passing over is a shifting of standpoint, a going over to the standpoint of another culture, another way of life, another religion. It is followed by an equal and opposite process we might call "coming back", coming back with new insights to one's own culture, one's own way of life, one's own religion.'[4]

In other words, 'passing over' involves at least two things: (1) an attempt to understand another's faith from within, standing as it were in his shoes; and (2) a return to one's own belief, all the stronger and richer for the experience.

What I am about to say therefore is not to be mistaken for the former, discarded, approach but is rather to be understood as pre-supposing the latter.

---

1 Cf. John S. Mbiti, 'Christian Education in the Background of African Traditional Religions' (mimeographed), paper delivered at the Annual General Meeting of the Christian Churches' Educational Association, Nairobi, Kenya, 19 September 1969. See also the writings of the Early Christian Fathers, e.g., Justin Martyr in his *Apology I,* xlvi, 1-4; II, xiii and Clement of Alexandria in his *Stromateis* I, v. 28. Clement, for example, sees Greek philosophy as 'a preparation, paving the way towards perfection in Christ'.

2 Kenneth Cragg, *The Christian and Other Religions* (Mowbrays, London, 1977) ch.I 'This Earth, My Brother', pp.1-16, esp. p.3.

3 See for example the method expounded by Ninian Smart in his *The Phenomenon of Religion* (Macmillan, London, 1973) and applied in his *Background to the Long Search* (BBC, London, 1977).

4 John S. Dunne, *The Way of all the Earth* (Sheldon, London, 1970), pp.xii-xv, esp. p.vii.

4. The Power of the Cross

All the world's major religions concern themselves with the problem of suffering. This is hardly surprising if we reflect that one way of defining religion is to describe it as man's response to his total environment, and one aspect of this environment, indeed a constant factor in life, is pain. If we are not trying to cope with sickness and death within the immediate family circle then we are being constantly confronted through the media by earthquakes, floods and drought in the so-called Third World and holocausts, violent and non-violent protests and cold wars in the so-called civilized world.

The different religions propose different solutions. Hinduism, for example, settles for 'illusion'. Only the other world is real, this world is illusory and must be transcended. Through countless numbers of re-incarnations or cycles of rebirth man will eventually be released from this world and absorbed into the All. Marxism, in contrast, settles for 'utopia'. This world alone is real and man in history will save himself by his own effort. A new society will be brought about by material means. Hinduism emphasizes the *spiritual,* Marxism the *material.* Christianity, to my mind, however, offers the true, the real solution. It is neither exclusively idealistic nor wholly materialistic but rather realistic. Christian faith both accepts and transcends suffering. It does so by means of the cross. In the cross we see God become man, taking on himself the suffering of mankind. Moreover, we see suffering redeemed become redemptive suffering; we see suffering transcended, as death the usurper is overcome by resurrection.

It is from the cross that the Christian ethic derives its power and motive force. Christians love because God loved. And for Christians there is hope in despair, joy in pain and life in death. 'We preach Christ crucified . . .' says Paul, 'the power of God and the wisdom of God' (1 Cor. 1.23-4).

12

2. THE CHRISTIAN ETHIC AND OTHER ETHICS

Having laid our foundations carefully and arrived thus far it is now appropriate to make a comparison between the Christian ethic and other ethics before proceeding to our ultimate objective of exploring the possibilities for ethical dialogue—at the level of living—between Christians and members of other religions.

1. Law of love or love of law?

Christian and Muslim concepts of law

There is a fundamental difference between Christian and Islamic ethics. One way of stating this difference is to say that Christians stress love while Muslims focus on law or that Muslims focus on keeping specific rules while Christians stress inner disposition. Another is to say that Christian ethics are ethics of the kingdom of God while Islamic ethics are community ethics.[1]

(i) Ethics of the kingdom of God

For Christians the law is summed up in the words of Jesus: 'You shall love the Lord your God with all your heart, and with all your soul, and with all your mind. This is the great and first commandment. And the second is like it, You shall love your neighbour as yourself. On these two commandments depend all the law and the prophets' (Mt. 22.37-40 and parallels). The first is taken from Deuteronomy 6.5 and the second from Leviticus 19.18. The first was rightly regarded as forming the heart of Jewish religion thus putting love for God right at its centre. The second was tending to be accepted as fundamental ethical teaching in rabbinic Judaism. But the distinctive emphasis of the unity of the two probably belongs originally to Jesus.[2] In short, Jesus initiated the Christian insistence on love as the fulfilling of the law (Mt. 5.17; Rom. 13.8-10; Gal. 5.14).

Yet the New Testament does provide us with a body of ethical teaching, often misleadingly called 'The Sermon on the Mount', in Mt. chs. 5-7. It is most likely to be regarded as a collection of the sayings of Jesus about discipleship delivered on various occasions and in different places. It is described very aptly by R. V. G. Tasker as a new 'law' prescribed by Jesus or teaching about the way men and women must tend to behave when they have become subject to the reign of God. It is 'no external code of rules which can be followed to the letter, but a series of principles, ideals, and motives for conduct, more akin to the "law" which Jeremiah foretold the Lord would put in men's "inward parts" and "write it in their hearts" when he established a new covenant with them (see Jer. 31.33)'.[3] And in the words of C. H. Dodd: 'The precepts of Christ are not statutory definitions like those of the Mosaic code, but indications of *quality* and *direction* of action which may be present at quite lowly levels of performance'.[4]

In sum, Christian conduct is essentially a response of love to God and an outflowing of that love to others (see Gal. 5.23-4 on the fruit of the Spirit) resulting in the fulfilling of the law.

---

[1] I am discussing Sunni or Orthodox Islam to which 80 per cent of the world's 500 million Muslims belong.

[2] I. H. Marshall, *op. cit.*, pp.443-4.

[3] R. V. G. Tasker, *The Gospel according to St Matthew* (Tyndale, London, 1961), pp.57-8. I do not mean to suggest either that the Old Testament ethic is loveless or that the New Testament ethic is lawless.

[4] C. H. Dodd, *The Bible Today*, p.84, quoted in Tasker, *op. cit.*

(ii) *Ethics for the community*

In contrast, Islamic ethics are more akin to the Mosaic code, to Old Testament ethics. Both tend to give specific rules rather than general principles. As Judaism has the Torah, so Islam has the conception of the Shari'a. The Shari'a is often spoken of as 'Islamic law'. Its foundation lies in the Qur'an (the infallible Word of God to Muslims) and in the practice of the community of Muslims during the lifetime of Muhammad, but its present form is the result of elaboration through the centuries. The Shari'a shares some of the features of modern laws yet it is essentially different from both statutory law and English common law. It is a divinely given ideal for the whole of human life, dealing not only with public order and the usual topics of legislation, but also with private morality, etiquette, personal hygiene and, above all, religious ritual.[1] In the words of Norman Anderson:

'Unlike any other system in the world today, the Shari'a embraces every detail of human life, from the prohibition of crime to the use of the toothpick, and from the organization of the State to the most sacred intimacies—or unsavoury aberrations—of family life'.[2]

(iii) *Kingdom/State*

To be a Muslim is to submit to God and that in turn means accepting certain fundamental religious obligations often known as the 'five religious pillars' of Islam: (1) the Shahada or confession of faith—'there is no deity but God (Allah), Muhammad is the messenger of God'; (2) prayer; (3) alms-giving; (4) fasting; and (5) pilgrimage. Over and above this the Muslim is bound by the Shari'a. In order to focus once again the difference between the Christian ethics of the kingdom and the Muslim ethics of the community it is worth examining Jesus' and Muhammad's ethical concerns. When we examine the topics raised by Jesus in his ethical teaching (Mt. chs. 5-7) we find him (as might be expected) concerned with issues of his time: murder, adultery, hatred and love, divorce, the taking of oaths, retaliation and non-resistance, the three pious acts of almsgiving and prayer and fasting, over-anxiety about life and judgment of others. When we examine the teaching of the Qur'an we find Muhammad also concerned with issues of his time: prayer and worship, legal alms or poor-tax, the fast of Ramadan, the pilgrimage to Mecca, marriage and divorce, inheritance, food laws, wine-drinking, usury and miscellaneous other regulations. On the one hand Jesus summons his followers to turn to God and announces the coming of the kingdom, forming a people motivated by love; on the other hand Muhammad summons his followers to submit to God, accept him as his messenger, at the same time founding a state, a community under the rule of law.

Muslims find it difficult to live in a state where they cannot keep the Shari'a. Christians find it difficult to confuse religion and politics.

Yet when all is said and done, in most of the circumstances of modern life the ideals and standards of Muslims are very similar to those of Christians—even in marriage the difference is becoming less as Muslims embrace monogamy and Christians accept divorce.

---

1 W. Montgomery Watt, 'Ethical Standards in World Religions: IV. The Teaching and Practice of Islam' in *The Expository Times,* Vol. 85, No. 5, Feb. 1974, pp.132-5.
2 Sir Norman Anderson (ed.) *The World's Religions* (IVP, London, 1975), p.114.

2. New birth or rebirth?

Christian and Hindu moral sanctions

'Better to do one's own duty [*dharma*] though void of merit, than to do another's duty, however well-performed. Doing the works [*karma*] that inhere in one's own condition one remains unsullied.' —(Bhagavad-Gita 18.47-8).

'Hinduism is a vast subject and an elusive concept' says Thomas R. Trautman, summing up very aptly popular misapprehension and scholarly debate. The term 'Hindu' is derived from the River Sindu (Indus) because the Persians referred to India as the land beyond the Sindu. And the term Hinduism is probably a generic term describing the diverse and complex religions of the people of India.

For our purposes, we shall be able to short-circuit the problem by considering the pervasive and almost universal belief in *karma* (action) and rebirth found in Indian religion generally and the related concept of *dharma* (duty).

(i) *Karma and rebirth*

All living things are in a continual state of flux *(samsara)* which entails passing from one life to another. And the goal of all human conduct is to escape the round of rebirths by attaining salvation—liberation, release *(moksha)*—thus achieving transcendent bliss or absorption into the All. According to the law of *karma* (literally 'action' or 'performance') every good action is rewarded and every bad action is punished. The results of our actions we may not know in this life but we shall certainly know the consequences, for better or worse, in the next. For, unless salvation is attained, the new life to which we shall return will be shaped exactly in accordance with the merits and demerits of our previous lives. This law of strict retribution may be looked on as impersonal, merciless, inevitable— as automatic as the law of gravity and part of the structure of the universe— or as the expression of God's will for humankind. In either case it may entail an animal becoming a man or a man becoming an animal or even a spirit. Reward or punishment, either, of necessity, follows the appropriate action.

But, we may well ask, what makes an action good or bad? Good actions lead eventually to salvation and bad actions ensnare one further in successive rounds of rebirth. And salvation is to be obtained primarily by knowledge of God and the self so that ascetic discipline and frugal chastity are necessary preliminaries to attaining consiousness of union with the divine and finally to absorption into that All: 'Thus joy supreme comes to the Yogi whose heart is still, whose passions are peace, who is pure from sin, who is one with Brahman, with God' *(B.-G.* 6.27). Here, we encounter Indian dualism: this world of matter is illusion *(maya),* only the other world, the spiritual, is real. To discover the inner self the outer self must be denied.

(ii) *Dharma*

So far, Hindu ethics appear to be individually motivated. However, they do possess a social dimension. It is to be found in the fulfilling of one's duty *(dharma)*. The derivation of the word *dharma* relates to cosmological order. Part of that order (to be maintained) is the caste system. Individuals must perform *karma* (actions) appropriate to their class. To that end guidance is provided in the *dharma* or system of Hindu ethical theory and practice handed down from generation to generation. Vices such as ignorance, lust, wrath and greed are to be shunned (B.-G. 16.4, 21) while virtues such as wisdom, purity, generosity, self-harmony, foolishness, austerity, goodness, non-violence, truthfulness, freedom from anger, renunciation, serenity, compassion for all beings, gentleness, modesty, fortitude, forgiveness, kindness and humility are to be pursued (B.-G. 16.1-3). And, incidentally, the doctrine of caste explains as no other can all inequalities of life and endowment, thus offering an answer to the problem of suffering—a satisfying theodicy.[1]

Unlike Hinduism, however, which sees the individual's conduct as dictated by the quest for salvation through rebirth, Christianity sees conduct as a consequence of new birth. New birth releases the Christian from the bonds of original sin and sets him free in Christ to live a new life by the power of the Spirit. It is in this vein that Paul assures the Corinthians 'If anyone is in Christ, he is a new creation; the old has passed away, behold, the new has come' (2 Cor. 5.17) and admonishes the Galatians 'If we live by the Spirit, let us also walk by the Spirit'. And at the same time he lists the lusts of the flesh: 'immorality, . . .' (Gal.5.19-21) and the fruit of the Spirit: 'love, joy, peace, patience, kindness, goodness, faithfulness, gentleness, self-control' (Gal. 5.22-3).

(iii) *New Birth/Rebirth*

So while Hindus strive for salvation through release from rebirth into another life Christians receive salvation through new birth in Christ and live a new kind of life. While Hindu ethics lay down rules for the attainment of personal liberation and the maintenance of social order, Christian ethics emphasize the qualities which characterize the life of a person living in communion with God and the implications for social behaviour.

However, we may still admit the similarity of standards in many areas of behaviour in both religions.

3. God's grace or man's effort?

Christian and Sikh motive forces

'*Karma* determines the nature of our birth, but it is through grace that the door of salvation is found.'—(Japji 4, *Adi Granth*, p.2).

Sikhism or *Gurmat* is one of the most recent of the world religions. According to tradition its founder was one Guru Nanak (1469-1539) and three distinct phases may be perceived in its evolution: the devotional system taught by Guru Nanak in the Panjab during the early decades of the sixteenth century; the structure of Panjabi society, particularly its rural and martial elements; and Panjabi history from the time of Guru Nanak to the present day, especially the formation of the Khalsa brotherhood and its code of discipline in the late seventeenth century.[2]

---

[1] For a useful article on Hindu Ethics see Father Bede McGregor, 'Ethical Standards in World Religions: II. Hindu Ethics in Theory and Practice' in *The Expository Times*, Vol. 85, No. 3, Dec. 1973, pp.68-72.

[2] On Sikhism see W. H. McLeod 'Ethical Standards in World Religions: VII. The Sikhs' in *The Expository Times*, Vol. 85, No. 8, May 1974. pp.233-7; also his *Guru Nanak and the Sikh Religion* (O.U.P., London/Delhi, ¹1968, ²1976) and 'Sikhism' in Whitfield Foy (ed.) *Man's Religious Quest* (Croom Helm for the Open University, London, 1978) pp.265-313.

The devotional teaching of Guru Nanak and the codes of discipline provide the basis for any discussion of Sikh ethics.

(i) *An inner discipline*

Guru Nanak's concern is the quest for salvation. God is one and although personal he is transcendent Creator, formless, eternal and ineffable. But he is also a God of grace and therefore knowable in some sense. He has graciously imparted to man a revelation in creation so that through spiritual awakening man may perceive his immanence in the world. This salvation depends both upon God's grace and upon the individual's own effort to cleanse himself of all evil, so appropriating the salvation offered to him. In his natural state man is in bondage to or attached to a world of unreality (maya), not to be understood as an illusory world but as a world of transient values. The result of this bondage is a continuous round of rebirths and endlessly protracted separation from God. However, God, because he is gracious, communicates his revelation to man in the form of the *sabad* (*sabda*, 'word') uttered by the guru (the 'preceptor'). Any aspect of the created world which communicates a vision or glimpse of the nature of God or of his purpose is to be regarded as an expression of the *sabda*. And the guru who draws attention to the revelation is not a human preceptor but the 'voice' of God mystically uttered within the human heart. Duly awakened by the guru, the enlightened man looks around and within himself where he perceives the *hukam* ('divine order' or 'harmony'). Salvation consists in bringing oneself within the patterns of harmony and this is achieved by means of a specific discipline which involves inward and deep meditation on the divine Name—the practice of *nam simran* or *nam japan*. The essence of the *nam* is harmony and through this discipline the faithful Sikh ('disciple', 'learner') progresses, passing eventually into union with God and release from the round of rebirths— salvation.

Lest it be thought that Guru Nanak's teaching was wholly individualistic it seems appropriate to quote a recently popularized summary of his teaching, 'How to Attain Perfection': the Guru teaches people, so it reads ,to (1) *nam japo* (recite the name of God); (2) *kirat karo* (do your duty); (3) *vandh chako* (share your earnings with others). Moreover, Guru Nanak condemned withdrawal from the world and encouraged the pursuit of work and normal family life. To this may be added equality, rejection of discrimination based on caste and tolerance towards others.

(ii) *The codes of discipline*

These are the marks of contemporary Sikh orthodoxy. They include the externals of the 'Five Ks', sworn to by the Khalsa brotherhood at baptism: the *kesh* (uncut hair), the *kangha* (comb), the *kirpan* (dagger or short sword), the *kara* (steel bangle) and the *kechh* (breeches which must not reach below the knee); and various prohibitions which include theft and adultery, gambling and intoxicants (abstaining from tobacco being the most widely kept and abstaining from alcohol the least observed), meat slaughtered according to Muslim regulations and piercing the skin for ornaments.

It is certain of these rules which cause Sikhs problems in contemporary society, so much so that they abandon many of the externals such as uncut hair and in so doing run the risk of being called 'fallen' by the orthodox. One small dissenting group within Sikhism—the *sahaj-dhari* Sikhs—does not honour the codes in their fulness but claims to follow the teaching of the Gurus (of which there are ten, Nanak and his nine successors) in their pristine purity.

(iii) *Grace/Effort*

When we turn to a comparison of Christian and Sikh ethics it is unnecessary to go into great detail in order to discern the distinguishing factors. It would appear that although Guru Nanak speaks of bondage it is a bondage which is broken by man's self-effort:

'This world is lost in temptation and attachment and is in great pain of birth and death.
Hasten to Satguru's sanctuary, repeat God's Name in your heart and be saved . . .
The waves of avarice and greed are overcome by the pre-eminence of God's Name in the soul . . .'—(Gujri Ashtapadi, *Adi Granth*, p.505)

And when he speaks of grace it is grace accompanied by self-effort:

'The grace of the Master is on those who have meditated on him, with single mind, and they have found favour in his heart.' —(Siri Ragu 27, *Adi Granth*, p.24)

Christianity teaches salvation by grace through faith (Eph. 2.8) with a fruit of good works:

'Religion that is pure and undefiled before God and the Father is this: to visit orphans and widows in their affliction, and to keep oneself unstained from the world.'—(James 1.27)

Perhaps the key distinguishing factor is that in Indian religion 'salvation' means release from a continuous round of rebirths and in Semitic religion salvation means deliverance in this world.

Yet once again, when all is said and done, Christian and Sikh ethics occupy much common ground, for example:

'Make contentment thine earrings, spiritual endeavour thy begging bowl and wallet, and meditation
Wear death like sackcloth, in manner of life let thy body be that of a virgin and faith in God by thy staff.
Let communion with all men be thy holy order, control of the mind means control of the world.'—(Japji 28, *Adi Granth*, p.7)
'Who is wise and understanding among you?
By his good life let him show his works in the meekness of wisdom . . .
The wisdom from above is first pure, then peaceable, gentle, open to reason, full of mercy and good fruits, without uncertainty or insincerity.
And the harvest of righteousness is sown in peace by those who make peace.'—(James 3.13, 17-18)
'Godliness with contentment is great gain.' (1 Tim. 6.6).

4. New man or new society? Christian and Marxist goals

I make no apologies for including Marxism among the religions. I do so for two good reasons: (1) Marxism is a good example of what may be called modern secular alternatives to religion which might be said to include positivism, humanism, Freudianism and sport; (2) Marxism possesses many 'religious' characteristics, to take Maoism for example: with its set of doctrines, code of ethics, plethora of rituals, experimental dimension and new order all it seems to lack is God and the transcendent but even that may be a question of definitions.[1] Says J. Milton Yinger: 'Prophetic condemnation of an evil world has a long religious tradition. Marxism as an ideology and communism as a movement can be seen as a modern secularized, and highly specialized, prophetic movement, proclaiming the road to justice. Where positivism sees science as the road to salvation, communism sees the creation of new economic and political structures as the way'.[2]

(i) Marxian dilemma

If we were to enquire of the man in the street the nature of Marxist or Communist ethics he would most likely reply: 'The end justifies the means' citing as evidence China in the fifties, Czechoslovakia in the sixties and Cambodia in the seventies.[3] He would have in mind revolution, invasion, mass killings and replacements of peoples in the name of constructing a new and better society with justice and equality for all. He would be correct in so far as he referred to Lenin who in 1920 declared: 'Our morality is wholly subordinate to the interests of the class struggle of the proletariat' but incorrect if he thought he was expressing the views of Karl Marx. For the young Karl Marx believed communist society would come about of necessity and it would be a spontaneous, artistic expression of human nature—external norms and obligations would disappear.[4]

Very quickly, of course, we have arrived at the root of the Marxian dilemma: that Marx's view of man, history and society—what purported to be a scientific analysis—should so readily have become an ideology, even a 'religion', and ideologies constitute an alienation. But was it not Marx himself who said in *The Communist Manifesto:* 'The ruling ideas of each age have ever been the ideas of its ruling class'?

(ii) Alienation

In everyday English usage alienation means 'estrangement'. In the German, Marx employs two different words interchangeably, the first emphasizing the idea of dispossession and the second the idea of something being strange and alien.

As we know, Marx propounded his theory of alienated man against the background of three important movements or events: the Industrial Revolution, German Idealist Philosophy and the French Revolution. Its

---

1 Ninian Smart, *Background to the Long Search*, p.266.
2 J. M. Yinger, 'Secular Alternatives to Religious Action' in Whitfield Foy (ed.), *op. cit.,* p.547.
3 Quoted by Eugene Kamenka in his *Marxism and Ethics* (Macmillan, London, 1969), p.57.
4 *Ibid.,* p.56.

immediate origins, however, appear to be twofold: (1) Marx's attempts to come to grips with Hegel's philosophy; and (2) Marx's reflections on man in society—as he observed him. The first is philosophical, the second is sociological. One could say that Marx begins with man and an idea and in strict scientific and philosophical terms he gets beyond neither.

For Hegel, reality was Spirit (mind, reason) realizing itself, producing itself, and alienation took on the meaning of the world failing to understand that it was not external to Spirit. In other words, alienation would cease and men would be free if and when they saw that their culture and environment were creations of Spirit. Marx disagreed, to him the external world was part of man's nature and alienation would not cease with its abolition:

'An objective being has an objective effect and it would not have an objective effect if its being did not include an objective element. It only creates and posits objects because it is posited by objects, because it is by origin natural.'[1]

So Marx affirms his belief that the external world is part of man's nature and man's vital role is to establish a right relationship with his environment. If Hegel had an idea of the Spirit as real then Marx has the idea that only man and the world are real.[2]

In his earlier writings Marx discusses several types of alienation: religious, philosophical, political and economic. It is to the last-mentioned that he attaches most significance and pays the greatest attention because, he believes, man's fundamental activity is work. Therefore I shall examine them in reverse order.

(1) *Capitalism* alienates. For Marx the outstanding achievement of Hegel's philosophy is that Hegel grasps the self creation of man as a process . . . that he, therefore, grasps the nature of labour, and conceives objective man (true, because real man) as the result of his own labour. Man's 'species-being' ('species-nature') is to be found in his creative activity, in his conscious transformation of the outside world. But man becomes alienated from his species-nature—from himself— when he loses the creative quality of labour through, for example, division of labour and mechanization. Man ceases to rule; instead he is dominated by the institutions and goods he has himself created.

(2) *Religion* alienates. Religion serves the double function of a compensation for suffering and a projection of man's deepest desires. It is a social projection. Man makes religion; religion does not make man. Religion is the 'imaginary realization of the human essence because the human essence possesses no true reality'. Religion must be abolished as a symptom of man's alienation. For 'in religion the

---

1 Karl Marx in David McLellan (ed.) *The Early Texts* (O.U.P., London, 1971), p.167.
2 E. Kamenka traces this to the later Feuerbach who, in his *Essence of Christianity*, wrote: 'There is no other essence which man can think of, dream, imagine, feel. believe in, wish for, love and adore as the *absolute*, than the essence of human nature itself' (*op. cit.*, p.15).

human imagination's own activity, the activity of man's head and his heart, reacts independently on the individual as an alien activity of gods and devils . . .'[1]

(3) *Philosophy* alienates. This is particularly true of Hegel's philosophy which reduces man and history merely to mental processes and replaces God with an Idea.

(4) *Politics* alienate. For politics, say Marx, had originally to do with people's real existence in history but soon became formalized into the State.

(iii) *Marxism and Ethics*

If Marxism is true to itself it must abjure any ethic. According to Karl Marx's philosophical pre-suppositions man is subject to no external standards, he is master of his own fate and moreover he provides the impulse of his own achievements. According to his scientific analysis man is subject to the laws of economic determinism and part of the dialectical process. In theory then there is no such thing as 'ought' but only 'is' and no imperative only an indicative. In practice, however, Marxism, neo-Marxism (call it what you will), has taken the form of an ideology or a religion, preaching justice and equality for all.

(iv) *New Society/New Man*

With regard to 'alienation' Christians and Marxists are in accord in so far as they both stress the importance of creative work. For Marxists it is because man's nature in so far as he is man is to engage in creative labour. For Christians it is because man is created in God's image with the mandate to rule and subdue the earth. They are in discord, however, when Marxists believe man can change himself by changing his relation to his social being, viz. by changing society, and Christians believe that alienation is to be abolished only through the sin-bearing Second Adam and a new creation. It is not a question of new society creating new man but rather of new man endeavouring to bring in a new society which will in turn nurture new man.

---

[1] Marx in his *Economic and Philosophical Manuscripts* (Paris, 1844).

3. ENGAGING IN ETHICAL DIALOGUE

1. Areas of Common Concern

On the basis of a common humanity, in fulfilment of God's purpose that mankind should subdue and rule the earth and in accordance with the Christian ethic of love, Christians not only may but must enter into dialogue, at the level of living, with people of other religions. But, we may well ask, where do we begin? I suggest that one possible starting place is within an area of common concern. As a result of the comparisons already made in the last section several such areas can be identified. They are: (1) *man in community*—man is created to live not only in relation to and in harmony with God and nature but also in relation to and in harmony with his fellow human beings; (2) *race and equality*—surely one of the most important questions of our century is whether people of all races and colours whom advance in science and technology have made near neighbours can live in harmony[1]; (3) *ecology*—there are vital issues concerning man's human and physical environments which call for attention in today's world; and (4) *development*—there is much suffering to be alleviated. All four areas involve the posing of ethical questions, the making of ethical judgments and the implementation of ethical decisions. However, I intend that we confine ourselves to a brief exploration of only one of them: the area of 'man in community'.

2. Man in Community

A rapidly changing technological world means considerable upheaval in terms of social order for all: old and familiar structures are passing away and new ones have yet to take shape. But for those of other religions in British society there exists not only the general sense of insecurity and bewilderment common to all but their own particular crisis of identity: they are 'immigrants' who have been uprooted from familiar cultural, religious and physical surroundings and transplanted into an alien culture on foreign soil. Into this category fall Hindus from East Africa and India, Muslims from Pakistan and Sikhs from the Panjab. And the first question to be faced with ethical implications is this: 'How can they learn to live with other men in community?'.

(i) Marriage and the Family

Marriage means many different things for different people. It may mean emphasis on romantic love between individuals or acceptance of arranged marriages reflecting kinship alliance. Yet whatever else marriage is about it is about children. And children need the security of stable family life in order to develop as whole persons. No member of any of the religions can be encouraged by the break-up of family life. However, Asians in Britain, of whatever religion, find it difficult to continue their traditional pattern of family life. Back home the household was most likely a three-generational unit comprising grandparent(s), married son(s) with their wives and children, unmarried, divorced or widowed uncle or aunt—the *extended family* as over against the nuclear family. Each member's position in the family comprised a complex of rights and duties and rules were

---

[1] Cf. Bishop Trevor Huddleston's talk in *Five Views of Multi-Racial Britain* (Commission for Racial Equality/BBC, London, 1978), p.68.

precisely and clearly defined.[1] But how could this continue in Britain, for example in the two-up-two-down *housing situation*? What rights then for Asians with regard to the structuring of family relationships and the provision of housing? The subject merits serious consideration for among other things the Asian extended family unit cares in exemplary fashion for its aged members, thus offering a salutary yardstick by which to measure British society's individualistic and perhaps selfish means of caring for its elderly. Another subject which deeply concerns the so-called 'immigrant' or 'coloured' members of British society is the problems encountered in trying to bring up *children*. Unlike their parents these children inhabit two worlds and move constantly between two cultures. In the home one set of norms prevails, in the school another. Often the home is too rigid and legalistic with regard to behaviour patterns, whereas the school is too tolerant and society at large is too indulgent and permissive. Dialogue is desperately needed in this area. I suggest it ought to begin with Christians taking the initiative in identifying felt needs within local communities such as the school, the community centre, the youth club and the housing association.

(ii) Employment and Work

We have already noted that Christians and Marxists agree on the importance of work for man's fulfilment. Moreover, Christians have a distinct work ethic. What rights then have the unemployed of whatever religion? Is it right that minority underprivileged groups should do all the late-night shift work in certain industries? Concern for humanization would suggest a negative reply and add the caution as to the effect on marriage and family life.

(iii) Education

Britain possesses a state education system open to all-comers. However, that provision in itself does not guarantee education. Is it right, for instance, that insufficient attention is paid to the language problems of 'immigrant' groups? Equality means equality of opportunity in real terms and this will not be achieved until linguistic and, derivatively, cultural barriers are surmounted. Naturally, Muslims and Christians, for example, will never agree on the same standards and practices as normative for society either in educational or other important matters. But it must be right that each should go as far as possible to meet the other's felt and agreed needs.

(iv) Law and Order

Perhaps the most frequently-cited example of a problem relating to the enforcement of law and order is that of the Sikh turban-wearer who refuses to wear either the bus conductor's cap or the motor cyclist's crash helmet. The reason he gives is one of religious duty. Perhaps in the first instance the issue can be resolved in terms of cultural awareness but in the latter instance this is not possible. The issue is a legal one and can only be resolved either by submission to the law, by relaxation of the law, or by some agreed

---

1 Cf. Verity Saifullah Khan, 'The Pakistanis: Mirpuri Villagers at Home and in Bradford' in James L. Watson (ed.), *Between Two Cultures: Migrants and Minorities in Britain* (Blackwell, Oxford, 1977), pp.57-89.

compromise. For Sikhs, however, the matter is essentially religious, although ethics on an individual basis are involved. For Muslims, on the other hand, such matters are essentially community matters. Muslim ethics are community ethics and living in a non-Muslim society poses particular problems. Consequently, while Christians and Muslims may agree on the importance of maintaining public order and morality they will differ radically about its source. The only solution open to orthodox Muslims is to demand separate laws for the Muslim community, for example separate marriage laws, different from those applying to society at large. What is right?

Discussion by the different religions of such ethical matters, many of which call for decision, must serve to sharpen issues between them so that from dialogue at the level of living will ultimately arise and develop dialogue at the levels of thinking and believing.